Journey to a Total Woman

By
Verna Steele

The Journey To a Total Woman

©Copyright 2013 by Verna Steele
All rights reserved. No portion of this book may be reproduced, scanned, or stored in a retrieval system, transmitted in any form or by any means -electronic, mechanical, photocopy, recording, or any other – except for brief quotations in printed reviews without permission of Publisher.

Please do not participate in Piracy of copyrighted materials.

Unless otherwise indicated, all scripture are KJV

Order today

Verna Steele
TheJourneyTATW@yahoo.com

Rivers of Living Water Ministries International
2948 W. Madison St.
Chicago, IL 60612
773-826-1442
www.rolwchicago.com

ISBN 978-0-578-12296-0

Printed in the U.S.A

ACKNOWLEDMENTS

Writing this book was a long and difficult process but the grace of God guided me through. Many people helped me along the way (directly and indirectly). Several encouraging words and nuggets that I've collected over the years were the greatest tools I could have used. God first you are awesome!!!

To my parents, James Tabor (Geraldine) and Lillie Steele for always being a voice of Love, correction and reason. You all have been vital to the way I view life and relationships, you taught me the value of love and building people.

To my senior leaders, Apostle Stephen and Prophetess Yolonda Garner thank you for seeing the potential in me when I was in a broken state. Your love, teachings, and persistence assisted me in taking up my bed to walk into purpose.

To my Captains Elder Aqua Robins and Prophet Phillip Harris – You two set me up for a sovereign surprise… I love surprises. Thanks a million for the opportunity to advance God's kingdom by way of the Prophetic and intercession.

To the children of my loins, Tamara, Terri, Samuel Jr. plus the ones that have placed in my heart as my own. Kordny, James Jr., Jacquez, Treli, Patsy, Keesha, and last but not least, Tiara. You all have verbalized and demonstrated your faith in me. You rock!!

To my Siblings, Ronald, Vanessa, Derrick, AQUA ☺ wink, Floyd, and James Jr. Thank you all for being who you are, a bunch of rare and creative individuals that have bought so much laughter, joy, and other kind of days! I wouldn't trade you for the last bowl of my Momma's famous banana pudding. Now that's real love.

To Apostle Daryl O'neil, you rock, you've been a great influence in my life. The small nuggets, hugs, and teaching on the real meaning of Love " GOD IS LOVE" the encounter with the unmarried ministry has changed my life.

To Terrence Blake Jr. AKA TJ Flow for your patience while going through the process of creating the book cover. Book cover number 6 was the winner.

To Laticia Strahan and Royce Strahan(millionaire man) for taking out the time to edit the book. You were so encouraging and patient with me. I love you both.

Also, My family and friends, The Brown family, Rivers, ANWA, VANRU , Women of Zion, Kidsdoc, and (TUM) The unmarried movement team Thank you all for your support, laughter and drive it means the world to me.

Table of Contents

Foreword	6
Reflection	8
A Virtuous Woman	9
Relationships	23
✓ Relationship with God	26
✓ Relationship with yourself	33
✓ Relationship with others	38
Emotions	45
✓ Fear	47
✓ Shame	53
✓ Blame	61
Deception	70
Doing things my way	81
Default status	89
Growing	96
Practice what you preach	100
Forgiveness	103

Foreword

Masterpiece-
A riveting tale of time travel to freedom.

The truth revealed from the desk of women all over the world, who didn't have enough courage to put ink to paper.

This is a message of Love that will smother pain, shame and Fear!!!

For the drowning this book is a lifeguard, for the blind this book is a guide dog, for the grief stricken this book is Hope.

Verna Steele has masterfully written a beauty for ashes portrait with an open window to place the picture of every women that reads it.

Elder Aqua L Robins
Rivers of Living Water Ministries, International

Impactful

Life has a way of bringing the strongest individuals to their knees. Past hurts and mistakes tend to plague our thoughts which lead to bitterness, rage and even medical conditions.

Pastor Verna Steele has captured the heart of God and written an extraordinary ministry tool.

Each chapter will cause you to receive revelation and encouragement throughout your journey to complete wholeness in Christ.

The prayers at the end of each chapter are power packed and life changing.

After reading this anointed book your life will be forever impacted.

Laticia Strahan
Author of "Waiting For Boaz"

Reflection

Pure excitement doesn't come close to how I feel in this season of life. What God has placed on my heart to accomplish leaves me speechless. I am beyond honored and grateful. This Journey alone has caused me to make major adjustments in my life, not just for me but for those that I am accountable to. My redeemer lives and He forever makes intercession on my behalf. It is my prayer that something said, shared; including all my dirty laundry that has been aired out in this book, will impact and encourage you on your own journey.

May the words of my mouth and the sincerity of which it's intended to reach deep within and change the way you view God, yourself and others. I pray something said gives revelation to some hidden agenda(s) and behavior. May you soar like an eagle and finish the course with extraordinary victory. It's reflection time.

STOP: Don't forget your highlighter and pen.

A Virtuous Woman

Because I am dealing with "The Woman," the most logical place to start this Journey is to go to the scriptures. The most talked about or utilized passage of scripture in the Bible when discussing a woman or when a woman searches for her identity they typically gravitate to Proverbs 31, "The Virtuous Woman". So much that to me for many it has become a common phrase and or a simple cliché.

Over the years, I have read this chapter several times but recently I've not only read it but also studied the contents of this chapter. I have sought God for revelation on this subject in particular.

Virtuous: conforming to moral and ethical principles, morally excellent

Synonyms: Blameless, celibate, excellent, guiltless, in the clear, incorruptible, pure, spotless, and untainted. After much prayer and meditation for insight regarding this passage, I realized that I had missed something so vital in this chapter. My perception of the virtuous woman was a learned behavior and perception that I adapted from the religious world.

This chapter starts off stating,

"The words of the king, repeating a prophecy that his mother taught him". Proverbs 31 was written by the king (a man) sharing the wisdom that his mother took time to reveal to him. It is my belief that Proverbs 31 was written by King Solomon and that Lemuel was a Pseudo therefore the Mother mentioned would be Bathsheba. I believe that Proverbs 31 was taught to the King from 2 different perspectives, two different stages of her own personal life

Proverbs 31:1-9 (Part 1)

1. The words of king Lemuel, the prophecy that his mother taught him.

2. What, my son? And what, the son of my womb? and what, the son of my vows?

3. Give not thy strength unto women, nor thy ways to that which destroyeth kings.

4. It is not for kings, O Lemuel; it is not for kings to drink wine; nor for prince's strong drink:

5. Lest they drink, and forget the law, and pervert the judgment of any of the afflicted.

6. Give strong drink unto him that is ready to perish, and wine unto those that be of heavy hearts.

7. Let him drink, and forget his poverty, and remember his misery no more.

8. Open thy mouth for the dumb in the cause of all such as are appointed to destruction.

9. Open thy mouth, judge righteously, and plead the cause of the poor and needy.

If Bathsheba is known for nothing else   she is known for her act of committing adultery with the king and this one action caused the death of many including her husband, Uriah, and her first son (unnamed). This act also caused the lives of many to be changed. Part 1 of this Chapter were words spoken from the wounded heart of a woman, wife, mother who had the burden of many upon her shoulder due to an act of pleasure. The woman she described to her son(s) in verses 1-9 to avoid is a reflection of herself. It's whom she observes when she views her reflection in the mirror. A woman overwhelmed with life's hurt, pain, shame and disappointments. Bathsheba saw herself as a woman that couldn't resist the lust of the eye or the desires of the flesh. The woman that she talked about was the woman she truly saw herself as. Think about that.

Proverbs 31:10-31 (Part 2)
10. Who can find a virtuous woman? for her price is far above rubies.

11. The heart of her husband doth safely trust in her, so that he shall have no need of spoil.

12. She will do him good and not evil all the days of her life.

13. She seeketh wool, and flax, and worketh willingly with her hands.

14. She is like the merchants' ships; she bringeth her food from afar.

15. She riseth also while it is yet night, and giveth meat to her household, and a portion to her maidens.

16. She considereth a field, and buyeth it: with the fruit of her hands she planteth a vineyard.

17. She girdeth her loins with strength, and strengtheneth her arms.

18. She perceiveth that her merchandise is good: her candle goeth not out by night.

19. She layeth her hands to the spindle, and her hands hold the distaff.

20. She stretcheth out her hand to the poor; yea, she reacheth forth her hands to the needy

21. She is not afraid of the snow for her household: for all her household are clothed with scarlet.

22. She maketh herself coverings of tapestry; her clothing is silk and purple.

23. Her husband is known in the gates, when he sitteth among the elders of the land.

24. She maketh fine linen, and selleth it; and delivereth girdles unto the merchant.

25. Strength and honour are her clothing; and she shall rejoice in time to come.

26. She openeth her mouth with wisdom; and in her tongue is the law of kindness.

27. She looketh well to the ways of her household, and eateth not the bread of idleness.

28. Her children arise up, and call her blessed; her husband also, and he praiseth her.

29. Many daughters have done virtuously, but thou excellest them all.

30. Favour is deceitful, and beauty is vain: but a woman that feareth the Lord, she shall be praised.

31. Give her of the fruit of her hands; and let her own works praise her in the gates.

Proverbs 31:10-31 is the description of the woman that Bathsheba was raised to be, the example of what the characteristic of a woman, daughter, wife, and mother should be.
The woman who Uriah desired and deserved and quite frankly thought he was getting when he paid the bride price. A wife and a woman her parents would have been proud of.
 "The Virtuous Woman", a woman free of shame, pain, or regret for her actions against God's law and disgracing her family's name.

Proverb 31:10-31 is a picture of the woman she didn't see when she saw her reflection in the mirror.

This was a plea, an expression of a mother's heart to her son(s) to assist them in avoiding the situations that could ultimately destroy a kingdom, and his ability to partake in a life of extraordinary living.

This Chapter speaks louder to men than women. It is a map, a pattern to not only having leadership qualities but becoming a successful leader that will impact and advance the kingdom of God. What was initially a bad situation became a mothers' testimony of righteous living to her children.

A, "Don't make the same mistakes that your parents made," warning. However, hearing the instruction is only a key, but applying the knowledge gives power. It's a vital point that a lot of people miss. In this case, we are talking about women, including myself.

Often times in life we are given instructions, truths, and lessons of life to adhere to and we fail to do for various

reasons. Some are the lust of the eye, desires of flesh and even a prideful heart posture. (1 John 2:16)
The description of "The Virtuous Woman" talked about the moral integrity of a woman, not her walk with God. For the sake of clarity, I do believe that the pattern that was laid out had to have been God inspired although it wasn't mentioned. I also believe that patterns and behaviors can be adapted by demonstration and many can walk out the process of a particular situation and never fully understand it. Simply doing and saying something because it was a normal pattern in your family, a learned behavior or the reason(s) why is far from the action.

I believe that the ability to truly accomplish the role and functions as "The Virtuous Woman", apart from the grace of God, will not be fulfilled. On another note, a lot of the characteristics mentioned in the Bible are the same characteristics I noted in women that assisted in raising me. I don't remember some of these women ever going to church unless it was an occasion. (Wedding, funeral)

Some of the qualities that the Virtuous Woman possessed are: She Prioritized, (planned and scheduled her time) she was respected, she had dignity, she was faithful, confident, she was called good and when mentioned she was known as an asset to her husband. She was not lazy but very domestic, loving, caring and fearless. Although all of these qualities are valuable, they didn't identify her as or make her a woman of God.

If we were to examine and compare ourselves to The Virtuous Woman, on a majority we would miss the mark severely. Thank God for grace! The point in stating this is simple: "Don't become a cliché, purpose to be whole." The woman that you've read about was trained to be many things to many people. The question is was she trained on how to be true to herself? I would say no. That's why you must see her for where she was and her cry was a woman's hope from a place of despair. Remember, we are taking this journey to become a total woman and in order to accomplish this we must be at PEACE (nothing broken and nothing missing) with the journey and the promise.

Knowing who we are as individuals and collectively will determine how long it takes us to get to this place called "Total". The tools required on this journey are, transparency with honesty, faith, diligence, and a made up mind. There will be some tears, some laughter and even some denial from time to time however, the end result will be to know who God says you are and be prepared for the sacrifices it will take to get there. This road to becoming a Virtuous Woman has been viewed from a deep religious place, when in reality it is simple. Love the Lord your God and be led by His words and not the desires of the flesh or the dictate and opinion of others. This realization has caused me to take my first steps into this journey; to really seek God for proper alignment, not just for marriage but for me to be whole and pleasing to the Father and assisting in the building process that will advance the kingdom of God.

Here are some Definitions for **TOTAL**

- Constituting or comprising the whole; entire; not in part
- Pertaining to the whole of something
- Complete in extent or degree
- The Whole; an entirety

The objective on this journey is to help identify the strengths that can be duplicated to advance the Kingdom of God and the weaknesses that can be strengthened by the power of God's word, through relationships, fellowshipping, and your ability to be transparent (honest) so that deliverance can be your portion.

A Prayer for A Total Woman

Father God, I ask for forgiveness in acts that I partook of for temporal pleasures. I ask for forgiveness for acts I performed in ignorance. I renounce all loneliness that would drive me to the arms of others. I renounce all the characteristics of the old man. I am a new Creature in you. I break the ties of all bloodline curses that would cause me to detour from your plan and promise for my life. I come out of agreement with old habits and learned behaviors that have caused me to be anything other than what you have called me to be and what your Word declares.

I pray that all negative traits of my past is only a testimony and not evident in my character. I am a demonstration of your word, and your word will not become a cliché. Lord, order my steps and give me strategies to set things in their rightful places, according to your Word. I declare I will be a woman that plans and prioritizes.

Teach me how to respect myself. Teach me how to be faithful and confident in all that I do in word and in deed, whether single or married. I pray that I am found to be an asset and not a liability. I pray that I am found to be that "Good Thing", according to your Word.

I renounce all man-pleasing spirits, and every voice that has had greater influence in my life than You. Lord, equip me to endeavor this journey and give me the Grace to embrace the process and see the finish. I pray for the strength to move successfully past obstacles. I will not be stagnated.

I will take this Journey from a place of wholeness and sobriety not from a place of being emotional or allow my thoughts to become obscured as the past hurts, pains and disappointments resurface. I will face them knowing that it's all a part of the Journey.

I pray for a transformation from the woman I am to the woman you desire me to become. I purpose to become the woman who was created in your image and likeness with the grace and strength to succeed.

Lord, I thank you for the confidence to move forward and not be paralyzed by life's situations and circumstances.

SELAH

Reflect on what you've just discovered and see what areas you need to improved

Relationships

I remember sitting in a Sunday service, the Senior Leader was teaching on the subject of relationships and being a relational person. I have prided myself on being a relational person, and a good balanced friend to those that I am in covenant with. I had to step back and examine myself and my motives in the relationships that I have and those I've avoided.

The message was sobering and rang out loud to me as he ministered, "*no one is exempt from needing people in their lives*".

The following are the relationships that everyone should have:

- Your relationship with God
- Your relationship with yourself
- Your relationship with others

Other relationships he mentioned, that I believe to be pivotal in developing balanced relationships with others, with different types of people :

- People who are more mature, intelligent, and experienced than you. These types of people will motivate and inspire you to grow.

- You can gleam from people that are on the same level that you're on. This will allow iron to sharpen iron.

- People that are not on your level, *never say beneath you*, can be inspired and empowered by you. Your assistance can help build their lives.

I listened to this intensely and realized that often times we do miss the forest for the trees. I realized that relationships are like currency, it should be a cycle of giving and receiving, pouring out of yourself and allowing others to pour into you.

A cycle that is constantly being replenished. Please remember that real, sincere relationships are not built or developed over night. It takes time, effort and energy. It is not a 1- 2 - 3 process. Be prepared to put in the work. It takes practice, discipline, consistency, time, and the guidance of God. With these applications, we will produce and maintain healthy relationships. Always remember that this process is never finished or perfected. As we grow and change, our ability to maintain healthy covenant relationships, every situation we find ourselves in will be developed. The reality of knowing that change is what it is, "change," helps us to function in relationships with God, others and ourselves. Having said that, get prepared for relationship elevation. Remember that it starts with you.

Let's talk about relationships.

Defining Relationship

- A significant connection or similarity between two or more things, or the state of being related to something else.

- An emotionally close friendship.

- The connection between two or more people or groups and their involvement with one another, especially as regards to the way they behave toward and feel about one another.

Your Relationship with God

you, refresh you in his presence, instruct, direct, and warn you when there is a need for warning? Ask yourself these questions: Do I really know God or know of him? Is he just my savior or do I know him as Lord, as Father, and as a friend? Do I have an intimate relationship with him or do I only attempt to communicate with God when I have a pressing need or when something great has happened and I'm thankful at the moment?

Only you can answer these questions. Do you have a relationship with God? Does your relationship consist of intimacy? Are you intentional about setting aside time to talk to your Heavenly Father and patiently waiting for Him to talk back to you so He can encourage

I know that this question is not a common question but it should be, especially when we are purposing to grow. This question is not an easy one to answer but it's one of the more important questions asked during this journey. This is a question that will cause you to take out the time to really ponder on the reality of where you are. If your relationship with God only consists of Sunday's worship services at your local assembly or your favorite television Pastor, Wednesday night Bible Study, where no one is really studying the Bible, your favorite gospel songs, chain emails and texts, the Facebook Evangelist or that occasional drive by through your Bible. O.M.G you are doing yourself a great injustice. Believe me when I say, this is not to judge you but to make you aware. The truth of the matter is that as I write this I'm faced with convictions of my own and the responsibility to reevaluate what I defined as relationships, as well. I am so guilty of some of these same things I write about, especially allowing the cares of life to get ahead of my time with God, myself and others. Although I had good intentions, the follow-up has not always resulted in what I truly desired. But, I'm endeavoring to do better and trust God's guidance.

One thing is for certain; relationships are built over a period of time. It's not something that you wake up one morning and have. The only way to develop a relationship with someone is to be intentional with communicating, with consistent and continuous dialogue between you and the person or persons that you are attempting to develop a relationship with. When it comes to developing an intimate relationship with God it all begins with getting to know him. The foundation of that Journey starts with knowing whom He is, His plan for you and the map that has been laid out for you in the illustration of His word.

I can't express enough how important it is to discipline yourself and purpose to become intentional about reading the word of God, studying the Bible, talking to God, purposing to become familiar with Him and His voice and practicing obedience. One of the results of getting to know Him will cause you to place your trust in Him for real. One thing I am certain of is that it's impossible to fully trust someone that you don't know.

Example: If a stranger walked up to me and stated that he is in trouble and needed to borrower $100, even if I had the money my answer would probably be no because I don't know him or her. *I might even be a little offended because he asked.*

However, if someone I knew, family or friend came with the same situation, my response would not be an automatic "No". I would weigh it and give the answer based on my relationship with the individual and availability. (Did I loaned them money before? Did they pay back? Were they honorable with the agreement, or am I willing to make the investment not caring about the return?)

My point is within relationships, we weigh the options. That's how it is with our relationship with God. If you don't know him it's hard to trust Him with your destiny, family, children, finance, spouses, business, employment, education, etc. You get the picture.

Bottom line is that we must have a personal relationship with God so that we will understand the terms that come along with our relationship with Him (ABBA) and trust His instruction in all that we do. I am a witness that His way works so much better than mine have. In the body of Christ we speak of covenant often and the covenant we mention is the covenant that God has made with us. My questions is, "isn't he worthy of us being in covenant with him?" If yes then why is there so little demonstration of our covenant with Christ? It goes far beyond our confession.

Another form of communicating and getting to know God is to communicate in the spirit, or speaking in tongues.

As a child I was raised under the umbrella of Holiness, C.O.G.I.C. (Church of God in Christ) One of the things I remember most about this time of my life was the power and presence I felt when my grandmother spoke in tongues. I remember being in AWE whenever she spoke. Without even stating that she was prophetic, she would speak into our lives and reveal to us what God was saying concerning our lives. (children and grandchildren). Although I had very little knowledge of speaking in tongues, other than it gives us the ability to speak to God directly and that the unknown tongue is not just foreign to many humans, outside of those with the gift of interpretation, speaking in tongues block the access of demonic beings and gives us a direct connect to God. Yep, that was how it was explained. As I grew older and the knowledge and understanding of God's word and the gifts that we have access to have become clear, I realized that one's ability to speak in tongues is a gift that God grants to all believers that desire it. It is the evidence of being filled with the Holy Spirit. He, not it, is the comforter, NEWS FLASH!!! It was not set aside for a chosen few. The ability to speak in tongues is a powerful tool (gift) accessible to all believers. It's a communication skill and a way to build your faith and develop an intimate relationship with God.

If you are a born again believer, and you do not speak in tongues, I strongly suggest that you go to the Elders or Leaders of your church and tell them of your desire to speak in tongues. It is a gift from God that He gives freely. If you have questions, if you don't quite understand the purpose and benefits of speaking in tongues, I recommend that you purchase,

"Benefits of Speaking in Tongues"

Apostle Stephen A Garner.
Rivers of Living Water Ministries Int'l
Chicago, IL.
There is nothing like having a relationship with the one that knows all and sees all. It has been such an awesome experience just to rest in that secret place and fellowship with the Father. I beseech you to make it a

priority to start building that relationship with the Father. On this journey make it your personal assignment to start building a new and exciting relationship with new vision, new purpose and new insight with God. Be intentional about really getting to know this God that you say you love and trust.

If you have strayed away or have not made this journey apart of your agenda in life, it is okay and it is not too late.
That's a part of the awesomeness that is available to us in Christ. To reflect, repent and move forward in the new. Thank God for his love, grace, and mercy. It has been my endeavor to stay connected to God and bring my cries, cares and issues before him. There is nothing like one's ability to communicate with the father of all fathers, the friend of all friends, the creator, the comforter, and the one that knows every hair on your head.

Sister, I am excited with you and for you. So get ready for a life changing experience and a well of information that will never run dry.

Your Relationship With Yourself

"Buy the truth, and sell it not; also wisdom, and instruction, and understanding." Proverbs 23:23

"To thy own self be true" –Shakespeare

When God laid it on my heart to write this book, I will admit that I rejected it for a long time. As time went on the burden for women especially unmarried women became so overwhelming to me. I knew it was time to obey and trust that if God says do it, then it will all line up. Too often I found myself frustrated with, in my own strength, putting my thoughts into words on paper. Finally I yielded to the Holy Spirit, set my fear aside and submitted to God's leading concerning this book and just began to write. When I got to this particular section of the book "Your Relationship with you,"
God began to speak and as I put the question out there I found myself realizing that one of the toughest, most thought provoking questions that I had to ask myself was, "Who am I?" That same question will probably be tough for you, "Who are YOU?"

In the process of putting this together I had to take out the time to really search myself for this answer. Most people would think that this is the easiest question, a no-brainer, right? But the fact of the matter is that it can be very challenging. The ability to be open and honest, transparent, is easier said than done, especially when it's all about you. After drawing a blank for an extensive amount of time, it really seemed like eternity, I didn't know how to quite put it. I found myself describing myself based on who others defined me. I was a long list of adjectives. WOW! I probably would have answered this question based on where I was at during that moment in my life, however challenging myself to think beyond that and being reminded that this journey is a self-discovery and it must be approached from a transparent place. Who am I? Am I just a mom, a wife, a grandma, someone's sibling, a member of a church, my parents daughter, a debtor, home owner, someone's friend or perhaps someone's enemy, even my own enemy? (inner me)

From my experience that is exactly how I would answer that question. I would be identifying a long list of adjectives. Other questions came to mind, behind the scene refusing to verbalize it. Do I have issues with myself? Do I talk too much? Am I withdrawn? Am I too skinny or over weight? Am I satisfied with what I see in the mirror or am I brutally critical towards myself? Am I more concerned about who people say I am, and how they believe I should be? Will the survey read: "oftentimes what I think of myself is not the prettiest picture painted?" The ultimate question is does who I say I am and who God says I am bare the same reflection?

This journey has challenged me to find the beauty within myself as an individual and not the characteristic or titles that I had adapted and attached to myself along the way. Now I can say the same to you. Have a talk with God and then encourage yourself in the Lord and watch this facet of your life take flight and you'll see yourself in a whole new light. If you ask me who I am today I would declare with much love and adoration and confidence that "I am chosen." After this journey you will know who you are versus who you think you are. Let's explore and discover that we can be so far off the mark concerning ourselves. Prepare yourself for a mind blowing discovery that you are wonderfully made and that you are an asset to those that have the honor of knowing you. I know from experience that the closer I get to God the vision of who I am becomes clearer. It's a liberating experience when God speaks and affirms to you that he loves you in spite of what you've done. It is important that you see yourself the way God sees you and the positive way others perceive you. Ask yourself, "How does God see me?" Not how my family sees me, nor my friends, nor the pastor, but God. What does He think of my actions, words, decisions, feelings, and thoughts? How does God see me?

Answer: He sees you as a son, servant, and friend.

SON

We're not God's sons by creation but by salvation. (Gal 3:22-26). He is our Father (Abba) and there is nothing that concerns us that does not concern him. As with your natural parents, there are times when we just refuse, neglect, and or sometimes avoid the plan and instructions that have been placed before us. Also, we find ourselves stuck, often times alone, or afraid to go to daddy and say I've messed up.

SERVANT

You are called to the service of worshipping the King of Kings and Lord of Lords. You are called to servant hood to model the principals of God's word and to advance the Kingdom of God through your public expression and demonstration. When this is done it pleases the King of Kings and Lord of Lords.

FRIEND

A friend is somebody who trusts and is fond of another. God wants us to trust and have faith in Him. He knows the level of Grace we have and the potential on the inside. He is our greatest FAN. Always thinking of what's best for us. James 4:4 states: A friend of the world is enemy of God. Even when we are hurting and uncertain about life's blows he still calls us friend.

Relationships with Others

Allow me to start by saying it is impossible to live a life without relationships. Even the Bible says, "It's not good for man to be alone." (Genesis 2:18) Often times I hear women verbalize that they do not desire friendships or relationships. One of the most common statements for women who struggle in this area of relationships is, "I don't get along with women." When I hear those words, immediately the warning signs are made ever so clear to me. "WOUNDED" When words are spoken they create something. If you've verbalized them over and over again, believe me when I say that you have now formed an allegiance with this declaration and you're warding off potential God ordained relationships. Don't fear, it is not too late to REPENT, RENOUNCE AND BE RESTORED.

Your invisible language, words you meditate on, speak louder than your desires and it says to others, "Don't talk to me", "I don't like people", and "I am not friendly." But the truth is that no matter how much you verbalize this, there is something on the inside of you that longs for relationships and constantly asks the question, "Why don't I have friends." The answer is *"you didn't want any."*

You've partnered with your souls' nature that speaks from a broken and wounded place that cries out it doesn't want friends, while the spirit man yearns for relationships. The end result is an internal struggle on the inside of you; a battle against the spiritual man and the natural man. Unfortunately, the natural man has a coach that trains and gives instruction and it's called your tongue. That small and deadly member in your mouth that has ruled over your heart and has made verbal declarations of negativity. Now your confessions have become a reality. Emotional confessions; "all people are the same; I know she, he or they have an agenda; I don't want to be hurt again." I have even seen cases where people have developed Pseudo, not actually having the appearance of, false, pretended, unreal, relationships with pets, spouses and sometimes their children to the point that the relationship suffers because someone is being suffocated by a person who is holding them hostage in an unhealthy, ungodly relationship that has no balance. The demand and pressure is simply too great. Even in marriages when a woman is unable to relate beyond her immediate family, spouse and children, this can cause a great strain on a marriage.

As a Christian/A Kingdom citizen that has entered into a covenant relationship with God, who is loving, relational and calls us friend, how is the position that you don't need nor desire relationships valid? What I know to be true is that oftentimes we embrace separating ourselves from people because of negative experiences that we've encountered in relationships. If you don't meditate on anything else on this Journey, I urge you, sister, to mediate on this particular topic with an open heart so that if you are one that has been wounded or perhaps guilty of wounding someone, by the time we're done exploring this topic you will have a new insight on relationships with a repentant heart, the necessary adjustments can be made. I know that the next question is, "*HOW DO I ACCOMPLISH THIS?*" The answer is allowing yourself to be comforted and healed from that wounded spirit, trusting God's instruction and seeking His wisdom. It isn't impossible. God desires to see you whole but most importantly you must embrace the healing process. Start with you and reevaluating your definition of who you are. How has your introduction to the others been, through a loving heart and with accepting eyes or automatic judging? Your assignment for this area is simple: REPENT, RENOUNCE, AND REBUILD.

I am not suggesting that you go back and find every relationship that you've had in your past and build from there; talk to God and He will give you instruction and direction. Remember that we all need people in our lives; even some of the ones that get under our skin and make us want to pull out our hair. If only to guide them in the right direction or so God can show us what could have been, and to pull us off those self-made platforms of *I've arrived*. If it wasn't for the grace of God, I have absolutely no idea where I would be and it frightens me to think about it. One thing I can say for sure is that in the midst of my storms where fear and uncertainty about my tomorrow was at its highest, is when God really showed himself as one who would never leave me nor forsake me, and most of those times it was by way of my family and friends. ☺

Prayers and Renunciations for Relationships

Father God, I repent for all verbal and internal vows I've made in the past regarding relationships. Words spoken prompted by hurts, pains, and disappointments. Walls that have been erected to shelter my emotions rather than being honest and transparent about the state and affect the relationships have had on me.

I forgive those that have spoken ill of me, those who I deemed cruel and unaffectionate toward me in relationships. I forgive my parents, siblings, friends, leaders, bosses, spouse and children for times where their actions and words caused me to withdraw and retreat from relationships. I ask for forgiveness for words that I've spoken to others in retaliation due to hurts, pains and disappointments that manifested in anger and rage. I now understand that hurting people, hurt others and I can no longer practice retaliation.

I forgive myself for not confronting situations head on, for wishing them away rather than verbalizing my expectations. I will be intentional in restoring fellowship and relationship. Lord, I decree I will be intentional about getting to know you in a more intimate way. I take full responsibility of my role to become a relational person and I embrace the process of change, growth, building, and maturing in the areas necessary, so I can have healthy relationships with those you have ordained to be a part of my life.

I break the Power of ungodly relationships, soul ties of my past and I purpose to establish new relationships under God's covenant. I serve notice to all negative emotions that arise to destroy covenant relationships and I decree they no longer have the power to accuse and judge the intention of others who display sincere love and fellowship. I renounce all the effects of past hurts, all past pains, all past disappointments, all self-afflicted abuse, all estranged relationships, especially with my parents and siblings. I renounce the voice of the stranger, which speaks louder than my confession of Love and adoration. I decree I will purpose to love and trust. I will purpose to communicate. As I take this journey of becoming the total woman, I will purpose to embrace this new beginning knowing that I can do all things through Christ who strengthens me.

I embrace Love and will not reject it and I am aware that this can only be done by embracing my relationship with You, with me and relationship with others. I break the power of dysfunctional relationships; I release my Spouse, Children, and friends from unhealthy ties in relationships. No longer will I allow emotions and past experiences to dictate my now and my future. I break the power of doubt and suspicion that I've developed over time to safe guard my emotions. I will no longer depend on my own abilities, but in all my ways I will acknowledge you, seek you, and trust you Lord to direct my path. Open the eyes of my heart so that I may see through the lenses of Godly fruit.

In Jesus name, amen

Emotions

When dealing with emotions it is impossible to generalize it because of the various emotions that we deal with on a day-to-day basis and in some cases, from one moment to the next. It's usually the negative emotions that overwhelm us more than anything; the danger of not having the ability to rule over your emotions can become a danger to yourself and others.

Because of unjust words and works done to us the old nature tends to rise up and wants to declare eye for an eye and tooth for tooth, but the greatest disadvantage is it tends to causes one to withdraw and live on our own little island When, in all honesty,

that behavior is not of God and the best way to rule over negative emotions is to meditate and apply God's word immediately, we tend to allow things to simmer and not deal with them immediately with the word of God.

"Be not be conformed to this word, but be transformed by the renewing of your mind." (Romans 12:2)

Emotion(s) can be defined as those heightened feelings, agitation or passionate behavior that can potentially knock us off the course of God's plan for our life. Be not mocked or deceived, emotions are real and can be a dangerous thing especially when we refuse to admit that they are evident- when we attempt to ignore what we feel as though it will go away; or when we spend more time dealing with our emotions as a victim and not a victorious woman of God with the ability to conquer situations and circumstances. Simply refusing to deal with negative emotions doesn't mean they will go away. It's when we refuse to deal with, to address, to serve them notice, the result of ignoring them is the very food that feeds our negative emotions and cause them to grow into bigger issues. Remember it is the small foxes that destroy the vines, vines of love, vines of patience, vines of strength, vines of communication and fellowship. The emotions we display should always exemplify the characteristic of a kingdom citizen. Our emotions should not rule us or stagnate the advancement of the kingdom of God or the Promise of God for us as individuals. Some of the emotions that we will deal with are emotions that typically hinder us from reaching the place of being total.

FEAR

Fear is an unpleasant feeling of anxiety or apprehension caused by the presence or anticipation of danger, a concern about something that threatens to bring bad news or results in some bad news.

Synonyms: terror, dread, horror, fright, panic, alarm, and apprehension.

One of the greatest emotions displayed is fear. Fear of the unknown, fear of being inadequate, fear of never being good enough, fear of being alone, fear of love because of lost love, and that's just to name a few common fears. Fear is real and an enemy to our growth and maturity. It also hinders our ability to fully access the things of God when not understood or diagnosed properly. Fear is not always negative; there is a reverential type of fear and there is a fear that halts progression and that's the fear we want to deal with on this journey. As I think about fear, and sometimes even the ability to confront and verbalize it, "I fear this or that." Writing this book has projected some hidden fears that I thought I had dealt with many years ago. One of the fears (apprehensions)

I struggled with, was taking my thoughts and putting them on paper. I was fearful that the readers would take note of my lack of education, the grammar, punctuations and format, but God in all his awesomeness brought back to my remembrance a biblical story that assisted me during this process.

(The story of Moses)

"Then Moses said to the LORD, 'Please, Lord, I have never been eloquent, neither recently nor in time past, nor since You have spoken to Your servant; for I am slow of speech and slow of tongue.'" (Exodus 4:10)

I so understand the fear he felt when he was given this charge; he was afraid to be a mouthpiece for God because of his speech, or lack thereof, but God encouraged him and gave him a solution in the midst of his apprehension.

So, I repented and pressed beyond that part of me and here I am, declaring by any means necessary. I will obey and finish what God has instructed me to do.

We are talking about fear, which is an emotion that preys on our personal insecurities and plays a scene over and over again. How do we move beyond fear? We must first find the root cause, the entry point of the emotion. In most cases it was verbally spoken, usually in our youth by someone we loved and trusted. Whether directly, indirectly or what you perceived. It can damage and alter the way you behave and deal with life and its situations.

I'm going to share one of my personal stories with you. Something sprung up in my memory while writing. When I was young, maybe 6 or 7 years old, my family was returning home from visiting my mom's parents. My dad was driving, mom was sitting on the front passenger side and my younger sister was sitting in the middle on the console. She was about 3 or 4 years old. She was playing a game with my father identifying facial parts. He would touch a part of his face and she had to identify it. I remember playing along mentally. Well, when my dad pointed to his Adam's apple and asked her "What is this?" mentally, I said *"Adam's Apple,"* and verbally she said, *"Your Esophagus, Daddy."* My daddy was so happy that she answered correctly. He gave her so much praise. He even told her she was the smartest girl in the whole wide world. That was the entry point of fear for me. After that incident I was afraid of public speaking and even answering questions in school. I failed horribly in the area of classroom participation because I feared not giving the correct answer.

Now, as an adult, I know that that one incident was designed from hell to cause me to not develop to my full potential. Eventually I realized that it was a statement made by a father to his child to encourage her learning skills, merely words of affirmation and it was never his intent to cause heartache and inadequacy to me. A lesson I wish I had learned years ago.

This is an example of the power of clutching fear. That's just one of my testimonies that I'm going to share. I'm not sure what clutches you, but if you think back into your yester years, I'm sure that you will realize that fear came in through illegal access and it's time to serve fear its eviction notice. For years and even now, most of my expressions are done behind the scenes, and with all the prophetic words spoken over my life and all the prayer that I received about the call of God on my life, I know that fear had more power than my purpose and promise. Today the keyword is HAD. I decided that in order to talk about the journey to the total woman, I had to take this journey myself and a part of the journey was facing fears. I am proud to say that I see the progress and so have others, including my leaders. I've received emails, texts, cards and even people approaching me, encouraging me to continue in whatever path I've decided to take because they noticed change in my life. Needless to say, those words have strengthened and encouraged me to go forth and continue to press forward. I tell you relationships make the difference.

"For God has not given us the spirit of fear, but of love, power, and a sound mind." (II Timothy 1:7)

This Scripture is powerful and in all honesty, most people have not been able to walk it out because they don't believe it. You know why? Because the fear is a larger giant than the truth of God's word. Although most people will never admit it, that's the only conclusion I could come up with. Repeated cycles in life confirm that conclusion. But when we are intentional about being spirit-minded people, we can embrace this scripture, *come out of the shallow waters and venture into the deep.* (Psalm 69:2) Remember that **F.E.A.R** is **F**alse **E**vidence **A**ppearing **R**eal. We are over comers and must stand bold in that declaration, saying, "I am fearless and walk in the liberty that God has given me."

SHAME

When I think of shame, I immediately imagine myself as a turtle hiding in its shell. The place that was designed to cover, protect and shelter the turtle.

Shame is a negative emotion that combines feelings of dishonor, unworthiness, and embarrassment. It has the ability to run deep, it can be a powerful silencer in your life and the brokenness of it often causes stagnation. It impairs the process of healing and growth. Although we often do not recognize it in ourselves, shame is an underlying drive for many of the things that we do and say and for many of the patterns we develop in relationships. Understanding shame and its role in our lives is the beginning of being able to face and overcome it. Until this happens, we will have far too many pseudo moments and days filled with fears wondering, "What if they found out I am weak," "I have failed," "What if people find out what I am really like" or "With what happened to me, they might not accept me." When I was a child around the age of 5 or so, at this time in life, my memories should have been filled with fun times of playing jump rope, my dolls, hop scotch or trying to ride a bike without training wheels. Instead of those wonderful memories, mine are filled with my fear of the next visitation. This was the period in my life when a relative was molesting me. A person my parents trusted to be a protector and caregiver. Something deep within told me that it wasn't right and that he should not be doing this to me, yet my body reacted and found this repeated act pleasurable over a period of time. Hearing conversations back and forth between adults, teachers and even other friends, I realized at an early age that it WAS NOT right. I am sure that is when shame took root and made its illegal entry into my life. Of course at the time I had no idea that what I felt was shame. I just remember being withdrawn and afraid to share; even when questions were asked, I wouldn't say anything. Some days I felt like it was my fault that it was happening to me. Other times I would feel as though I needed to allow this to continue or he would touch my siblings or other relatives. Sometimes I would be ready to tell my natural daddy, and that voice would remind me of what he would say, *"If anyone ever touches you there, let me know because I'm going to KILL them."* So I didn't tell because I didn't want the police to take my daddy away from me and have other people angry with me. It was indeed a shameful place for a longtime and a burden that no child should have to carry. I don't know when the abuse stopped, I would say at the age of 9 or10, but it magically disappeared and a desire had been awakened in me. It was a sexual appetite that I couldn't define at the time, creating a new place of shame. By the age of 13, I was pregnant and by 18 the mother of 3 children. Everywhere I looked I was being verbally abused by people I loved, who verbalized over and over again that they were ashamed of and disappointed in me. Then there was my mother, who didn't say a word. She would only shed tears. Those tears spoke louder than any words could ever have. They said to me, "I am ashamed and embarrassed." Other relatives and even some teachers verbalized their disdain, and had no problem telling me that I, the little girl, wouldn't amount to anything because I was too fast, saying, "You're only a pretty face and a nice body." That brought more shame. At some point, my shame had married hopelessness. I began to believe the words that had been spoken over my life. I looked up and had those children by a man who had promised me a house, minivan, a dog and a swing set in the backyard for my children and he was on drugs and nowhere around to assist me. In the process of it all I was forced to drop out of school to do what I had to do. Adding more shame. The infamous "I told you so" was screaming at me from every corner of my life. One day I decided to take over, make every word spoken about me a lie. I would control what happened from here on out. I thought the control would have victory over all the shame I had experienced in life. I traded the pain of shame for pride and control, and by the age of 25, I had broken the heart(s) of every man that said they loved me. I was verbally and physically abusive to most of them, sold drugs from the choir stand at church, had a prison record and witnessed so much violence it is a wonder that I can sleep at night. Talking about out there bad, I was now so full of anger, rage and I didn't care who was affected by the behavior because no one cared how they affected me or so I thought.

Around the age of 25, I met a woman who loved the Lord and asked me to go with her to a women's prayer meeting. It is where my life was severely challenged and changed. It's where my introduction to the apostolic and prophetic came. This woman, who I love to this day, my mother of Zion, would consistently tell me about the love of God, the plan of salvation and my relationship with God, not just going to church. One day at the prayer meeting, she began to apologize to me for all the hurt, pain and shame that I had experienced. The sexual abuse, verbal abuse, acts of violence. She never made me feel ashamed. When I asked her about it, she told me that my past is under the umbrella of salvation. I remember being on the floor crying and she rocked me and said let it go… all that shame that accessed your life illegally, and for every negative word spoken or thoughts that lingered in my mind, she released Christ there. For shame, she released victory and the spirit of an overcomer. For hate she loosed love; for deception she loosed wisdom; discernment and love of the Father that would never leave me nor forsake me. I remember getting up off that floor after being down there for hours and feeling like a new human being. I traded my shame for the testimony of Christ. I tell you that when the truth of God's word is demonstrated in His people there's a healing that takes place and drives you to be better. Yes, we are talking about shame, years of being in bondage to shame over things that I, personally, didn't have control over. I am so glad that someone obeyed the voice of God and spoke words of healing, breakthrough and deliverance in my life. The thing about all of this is that it was at that moment that I remembered the sexual abuse as a child, somewhere it was buried, but when I gave my life to God, FOR REAL, and petitioned his throne room for peace, my past was revealed to me in dreams and it was all so clear to me. I had to relive the pain in order to confront the shame. That's when freedom came. Now, my shame has become a testimony of healing at the hands of a loving father (Abba). Now, this might not be your story. Your shame might have a different face than mine, and I'm sure if you take some time to really search, some old wounds that you might not want to revisit may surface, but in order to deal with the shame, there will be some pain. Your shame might be homosexuality, lust, alcohol, drugs, mental or physical abuse. Or, it might be an inability to have healthy relationships short or long term, just to name a few. But the good news is that the liberty that you gain, once you make the necessary steps to becoming a total woman are well worth it. Gaining His peace that surpasses all understanding is one of the greatest tradeoffs imaginable.

Sometimes your shame is private and although you attempt to outlive and outrun the memory of it, usually you just can't, whether your shame is molestation, rape, abuse (verbal, mental, emotional) or lack of achievement or maybe a handicap. I can guarantee you that somewhere in the back of your mind, the adversary is playing crazy vivid episodes of your past to make you feel like it's all your fault. He even tries to convince you that everyone is witnessing it like it is engraved on your forehead, "RAPED, REJECTED, USED, And ABUSED." That is not the case. The truth of the matter is, although you've been victimized, you must give up that position as a victim. There is healing for you. Or maybe your shame is divorce, fornication, adultery or being a convicted felon due to bad choices made. No matter what type of shame it is, whether it is internal or external, it can be very painful and unless you deal with it, it will hinder the process of becoming total.

Being a person that is naturally drawn to people, both men and women, I have encountered so many different hurting people; some that I consider strong, weak, over the top, timid, rejected and some I have literally avoided. Having heard the stories of life, abuse and some so familiar to my own, I've wondered, "How are you still in that state and haven't moved on because surely, I have." How off the mark and wrong was that thought? Thank God for intimate relationship and fellowship. His wise counsel has assisted me and shifted my thinking. My ability to process things is totally different. I realize now that trauma affects people differently and no two people's reaction will be the same. *Jesus, I'm glad you're on our side, loving us beyond our faults and our needs.*

As I was researching shame, the reviews, articles and other material, a lot of what I received seemed very shallow in nature so I decided there's only one place to go: the word of God. Before I could finish the thought, the story of Adam and Eve came to mind.

"And the eyes of them both were opened, and they knew that they were naked; and they sewed fig leaves together, and made themselves aprons. (Genesis 2:7) Could it be that this act of seeking wisdom outside of God's provision is what opened the door of curiosity and the act of disobedience, opening the door of shame? Do you

realize that the first thing that they did was COVER THEMSELVES.

"Teacher, this woman was caught in the act of adultery." (John 8:4)

This story speaks of the woman that was caught in the act of sin, and was about to be stoned to death. Jesus, being who he is, knelt down without saying a word and began to write in the dirt "LET HIM WHO IS WITHOUT SIN, THROW THE FIRST BRICK." Verna's translation, "go ahead and bust her head." That's how we will often feel right? But in most cases we are talking about ourselves.

In the story of Hosea, he was in love with a whore. You know the story. That must have caused great shame, especially when she gave birth to another man's child.

One thing is for certain, whenever shame was revealed in the bible, it was the hand of God that brought strength and healing to those that experienced it. I am sure that there are more stories to validate my claim and the conclusion of it is you are not alone. Healing is available. It is made accessible to you when you truly understand that God loves you and has already placed your shame on the Cross.

BLAME

For some of us, there are seasons in life when we look around and we can think of hundreds of things we could've done with our lives and some of the decisions that we've made. We think of "If I could've, would've, and should've" and the voice of blame begins to whisper ever so loudly in our ears. The fantasies come in to play and we find ourselves with a long list of who to blame. "IT'S YOUR FAULT THAT I DID/ DIDN'T DO _____." Only you can fill in that blank. We blame ourselves, parents, teachers, spouses, children, siblings, and SO-CALLED friends and whether we admit it or not, we even blame God for some of the current places we are in whether it is geographically, educationally, mentally or spiritually. When I think about all that I desired as a child with no direction, now as an adult, I realize ideas are just that when there is no planning and structure put into play. I am learning even at my age that it takes more energy to point a finger, to walk in the inability to forgive and to be bitter than it is to simply let go and move forward in a new direction. I was thinking about in the book of Genesis when Adam was placed in the Garden, God gave him instructions on do's and don'ts. He had more freedom in the dos than don'ts.

I still wonder sometimes whether or not Adam fully explained the rules and rights to Eve or did he just assume that she knew to simply follow his lead. You know, if I don't touch it, then you shouldn't touch it either. All I am saying is that when temptation came, Satan went to the weaker vessel and I personally believe that he played on her weakness (lack of knowledge, her being uninformed).

She ate of this fruit and nothing happened. She offered the fruit to Adam and when he ate, things changed! Mindsets shifted; when the one with dominion ate, THEIR EYES where opened. Shame entered and then blame from emotions of anger. Adam said with much aggression, "The woman you gave me; gave me the fruit to eat." (Genesis 3:12) Being the head, he didn't take responsibility. He shifted to blame. That blame can be an ugly beast in our life and relationships. We must not blame others for our lack, inabilities and so forth.

We can no longer be angry at the sex offender, the absent parents, and the siblings that wanted to be a child and not have the responsibility of taking care of the sibling that is only 2-3 years younger. We can no longer blame our children for choices we made being teen mothers. We can no longer blame God who clearly gave direction, gave a road map that will take us to Destination: **Promise**. We can no longer blame the husband that was just as bound up as we were when we said, "I do," without seeking counsel, or the boyfriend who was just that- a boy forced to put on men shoes before time.

I remember being 13 years old and faced with telling my 15-year-old boyfriend that we are about to be parents. He was scared, but excited, and because his father was absent, he looked at it as an opportunity to be a better man or father than his own. Although he had big plans and great intentions, when the time came and reality struck hard his verbal declaration couldn't measure up to the responsibility of being a father. And by the time we were 18 and 20 we were parents of 3 and the relationship was a mess. I no longer liked him nor desired to have a house, minivan, the back yard with the swing set, or the cute dog for the kids to play with him. I couldn't stand him. I blamed him for messing up my life. I was fairly smart and could have done something with myself, could have had my own. I decided to quit school and take care of those babies, and I looked up and my kids' daddy was a drug addict. Are you kidding me? He was gone and messed up my ideal of a perfect life. My chance to separate from my dysfunctional family, my opportunity to once and for all make all the negative words spoken about me a lie and tell them "you were wrong about me and mine," was gone. After that, the blame list was longer than my DO NOT FORGIVE THEM LIST. After much prayer, study, intimacy with God, and being under healthy leadership, I now realize that my thinking was twisted, and now that insight has been made available to me, as a kingdom believer, and lover of God's word. I have been through major mental reconstruction and I've been on a journey of forgiving, that journey of accountability, and rebuilding relationships.

A few years back, the father of my children was robbed and beaten. He was left in a pool of his blood to die. He was in a coma for a few days and this process was long and painful for him and me. During his time of rehabilitation, we spent a lot of time together and were very honest about our relationship and our children. A lot of the blame, shame and inability to forgive were put to rest. I am extremely happy to say that after 20-25yrs of drug abuse that he is sober and I am trusting God to do some great things in his life. I do attribute some of it to our verbal declarations to forgive one another for the hurt, pain and blame.

PRAYER AND RENOUNCIATION FOR FEAR, SHAME AND BLAME

Father God,

I thank you for your word that goes out to accomplish its purpose and cannot be voided. I thank you that according to 2 Corinthians 5:17 "Therefore if any man be in Christ, he is a new creature: old things are passed away and behold, all things are become new". I renounce all negative emotions that try to water down your word and overwhelm me. I know that negative behaviors not only affect me but others. I repent for every negative word that I've spoken in ignorance, fear, hatred and anger.

I renounce every negative word that has been spoken over my life in ignorance, fear, hatred, and anger. No longer will the old man govern my behavior. I decree that I will meditate on your word day and night according to Joshua 1:8. I come out of agreement with all negative emotions that will have me to verbalize anything other than the truth of your word.

I cover my mind with your blood and I guard my heart with all diligence. I will govern myself accordingly and practice releasing the fruit of righteousness and love. I am aware that death and life are in the power of the tongue: and they that love it shall eat the fruit thereof.

No longer will I allow the emotions of fear, shame and blame to hinder the purpose of God for my life. I will seek you for instruction and direction in all areas of my life. Every heightened feeling, agitation that knocks me off course of God's plan in my life, I serve you notice. Your voice is no longer louder than God's truth and promise for my life. I will no longer ignore or run from confrontation and allow my emotions to run havoc in my life.

I will no longer deal with my emotions with the mentality of a victim but as a conqueror knowing that I can do all things through Christ who strengthens me.

I will no longer fear the unknown nor possess fear of inadequacy, fear of not belonging, fear of not being loved, fear of the opinion of others toward me, fear of communicating and walking in the identity that God has given me.

I will no longer allow shame to hover over my life. My past experience, shame that brings me dishonor, shame that silence the truth because it whispers my past or plays back behavior and situations that silenced me. Real shame and false shame no longer have a voice in my life. "I am crucified with Christ nevertheless I live. Not I, but Christ lives in me: and the life I now live in the flesh I live by faith of the son of God, who loved me, and gave himself for me," according to Galatians 2:20.

I renounce seasons of blame, where I live in a place of condemnation and blame myself for things I had no control over. I renounce the spirit of blame where I held hurt, pain, anger towards others. I stand on the promises of God and decree that I am whole and at peace with my past. My confession of faith is that I am wonderfully made in God's image and I live a life with nothing broken and nothing missing. I release myself, parents, teachers, spouse, children, leaders, friends and enemies from the strongmen of blame.

I decree that the spirit of God goes with me because where the spirit of the Lord is there is liberty .In Jesus name, Amen

DECEPTION

Practice of misleading somebody: the practice of deliberately making somebody believe things that are not true; something intended to mislead somebody: an act, trick, or device intended to deceive or mislead somebody.

Synonym: dishonesty, Trickery, Ruse, Sham, Fraud, Con, Cheating, Duplicity, and Deceptive

1 John 2:15-17 (MSG)

"Do not love the world's ways. Don't love the world's goods. Love of the world squeezes out love for the Father. Practically everything that goes on in the world—wanting your own way, wanting everything for yourself, wanting to appear important—has nothing to do with the Father. It just isolates you from him. The world and all its wanting, wanting, wanting is on the way out—but whoever does what God wants is set for eternity."

Let's **NOT** deal with Deception from the standpoint of being victimized at the hands of another. Let's deal with it from a place of self-deception. A place that we rarely visit if visited at all.

I am all too familiar with this place and it has taken a lot of bumps and falls in order to get to this place of growth and maturity.

In life, we create fantasy places and spaces. Our introduction for happily ever after comes at a very young age. We are presented with an ideal of family via the baby dolls, Easy-Bake ovens, kitchen appliance sets, the fake vacuum cleaners, and the makeover items. For some of us, at an early age, the fantasy places and spaces were destroyed by dysfunctions of all sorts. These dysfunctions distorted what we believed versus what is achieved.

I can remember having dreams, visions and being very ambitious at a young age. With all that I desired to accomplish and achieve, there were forces and incidences in my life that weighed heavy on my ability to see my dreams fulfilled. To have a plan, a goal and see it from an unrealistic place is one of the greatest heartaches to endure. I can remember spending time clearing my mind and healing from relationships that were dissolved.

Baby daddy on drugs, another boyfriend sentenced to 56 years in prison, another murdered, and others I just realized weren't "It." At some point I realized that I needed to take some time to just reevaluate my life, my decisions and to ask God to help me and give me clarity in the area of relationships. I remember telling God that I didn't want to be alone and how I refused to be someone's other woman or be with a man that is unstable. Well, I literally put a list together and I did so based on a lot of things, especially:

Ask and it shall be given
Seek and you shall find
Knock and the door shall be open to you.
So I asked;

I created this list:

- 6ft tall or greater
- Slim but not skinny
- Good steward over what he has
- Loves the Lord in deed and not just in word
- Gainfully employed
- Not cheap
- Love me, for real
- Educated/informed
- Well-dressed or opened minded enough so I can make adjustments, if necessary
- Sexually compatible
- Longevity ☺
- Sociable
- Cleans
- Cooks
- A great friend
- If he can sing or play an instrument that would be an added bonus
- Ok with him having children because I'm not having anymore
- A good father
- Loves family

This was my list and there was very little room for deviation. So about two years after this list was created (while I was in church and loving the lord), a friend of mine called me regarding business and informed me that she met this man and that she remembered a conversation that we had and my interest in what he offered. I talked to him a few times over the phone and decided to meet. Because I am cautious, I took another sister with me. Arriving before him to the meeting and waiting, I looked out of the window and saw this man approaching the restaurant. I looked at my friend and stated "OMG, that's him." (I had never met him before nor did I know how he looked). My friend (sister) asked me how did I know and smiling from ear to ear I said, "I can't explain it I just know that it's him." And when he walked in the door she called his name and he answered and introduced himself.

The meeting went well and he invited me to attend another meeting. I declined because of an engagement I had prior to the invite. A few weeks went by and I could not get him out of my mind. On the morning of my appointment at around 6 a.m., I received a call. Knowing who he was from the caller ID, my heart skipped a beat. He stated that he was calling to check on me and to pray that all went well for me. So, immediately, I challenged my list. "Ok, go ahead and pray"... He laughed and said, "You want me to pray right now?" And of course, I replied, "Yes." He prayed for me and I hung up, feeling he's a special man. A few days later he called back and stated that he was a little upset with me because I didn't call him to let him know how the appointment went. I didn't know that I was supposed to so of course I laughed and apologized; and from there a relationship was formed.

We began dating and he was (is) an excellent man to spend time with; always attentive to my needs and making sure that all my needs and desires were met. After a short period of sharing, caring, getting to know him, and YEARS of being free from fornication, I fell, and I fell hard. Between him living at my house and me at his, we were together at a minimum of 5 days a week. Soon after, I confessed my love and he was frightened by that and by the end of that week, he ended the relationship.

Because I come from a family of very headstrong women, I walked away. We decided in the beginning stages that if we didn't work out, there would be no drama. We would both bow and exit stage left. And I honored that agreement. It was a very painful place and space in time. Very strong women raised me and the motto is "never let him see you sweat," and I didn't. You don't cry over spilled milk. Just go get another galloon.

Weeks later, right before Christmas, a heightened time of a year when the single Christian women tend to feel a little more down and alone than usual, he shows up. There was a death in my family and everyone was meeting up at my mom's house. A lot of out-of-town relatives were in town for the funeral and I got a call from my mom stating someone wanted to see me at her house. So, when I got there, I immediately heard his voice and went into shock, thinking "Why is he here? Why are all the women in the dining room around him making him feel important?" (SMH) Remembering, he's the perfect gentleman and a great charmer. I greeted him and he asked if we could talk. I remember him saying, "Let's go sit in my car" and I declined and stated, "We can sit in mine." We went through the formalities and he expressed the void of my absence and the friendship we had developed. He wanted his friend back. And of course, I declined, not responding to his attempts until the month of my birthday when he put on the charm, HEAVY.

Sending gifts and apologies daily, he finally showed up at the door, took off his (my) favorite hat and placed it on my head and told me once again, "Please take me back." He won! Within a month later, we were living together as the perfect couple. Condemnation was so heavy until I was too ashamed to go to church. We were living as a married couple, the perfect couple that everyone hung out with; doing everything from praying, cooking, and cleaning to entertaining together. We even gave counseling with some of our friends.

Over a period of time, I was feeling the separation from God and the intimate relationship that I once had. I began to put the pressure of marriage on him again; he fought tooth and nail declaring that he had given me all that he was able to. He was divorced and made an internal vow never to be married again. The thing is that in all I've shared, I neglected to tell you that he told me in the beginning that he would never marry again, and I thought that it would change. I had thoroughly convinced myself that he was mine and that God gave him to me.

The checklist was completely checked off, including the ability to sing and play a keyboard. I prayed and asked God to change his mind. I loved God and that man and I didn't want to lose either one (self-deception and witchcraft). As time went on, he was firm in his stance not to be married and stated that God knows his heart. Things took a turn and I was intentionally picking fights and trying to force his hands. Pouting, crying, and reasoning with him. No go! And eventually I became complacent and didn't argue but I spent so many nights crying, "God I don't know how to get out." So finally one night I was in bed (next to him) and I heard the voice of God say, "Choose ye this day who you will serve." See, I had been waiting on God to do something and all the time it was up to me (deception). Finally, after a few minutes of thinking, I woke him up out of his sleep to tell him it was time to end the relationship and that he had to move. Of course he took that hard but he honored my love for God and he left. (The move was done by the end of the week, because any longer I would have changed my mind and been in it longer).

I convinced myself that because I obeyed God, he would run back stating that he would marry me because he couldn't live without me. And years later, he has not made that declaration. Please understand that this relationship was not as cut and dry as it seemed. After the relationship ended, the soul tie hadn't and for a while I found myself falling into sexual sin with him annually. I kid you not! Each time it was as though we were never apart. But one
day I cried so hard and I refused to ask God "Why?" this time. I knew that I had to break the tie for real and never look back. It was one of the most difficult periods of my life but a decision that I had to make.

Deception is real; self-deception is real and dangerous. I'm grateful to God that He kept me and He continues to keep me in all my doing and foolishness. The bible talks about counting the cost. My heart was the wage in this case, yet as time went on and I continued to stay in God's presence and being intentional about doing it God's way, I gained much wisdom concerning decision-making and I know now that even in the midst of this relationship, there was nothing deceptive about his actions.

I wanted to be angry with him. I wanted to blame him for robbing me of those years, but the truth of the matter is, I deceived myself and I had to take the blame for the decisions that I made. Sisters, don't be deceived or mocked. Don't do things in your own strength and ability. Do it God's way and in God's timing. His mercy endures forever and ever more. Don't try to do it in your own strength. Be careful not to see the forest and the trees.

Doing Things My Way

Because of misguided decisions, I found myself in situations that altered my life and even the lives of some of the people I love. In 1990 at the age of 22, I was a part of a circle of people who sold drugs, gangbanged and carried heavy weaponry. I encountered people, places and things that some only encountered on TV and movies. Never in a million years did I think I would be caught up in this lifestyle because it was totally against what I knew to be righteous or the plan that I personally had laid out for myself. Because of many buried emotions, the lust of the eyes and the mentality that I had developed because of broken dreams and flawed desire to achieve and succeed by any means necessary had my view distorted. I saw how that lifestyle worked and was able to pick apart the errors that many of my family, friends, and foes made in their attempt to hustle. I was strategic about working a plan. The devil showed me the glitter and glam of this lifestyle and somehow the seed was sewn that I could do it; I would be successful (it was as if the devil took me on the mountain top and said " Bow before me and I will give you the keys to the city," and I bowed.

I felt that because I was honest with my mom, that God would have mercy on me. I convinced myself that because I took care of several families that I was not a horrible person for selling drugs. Although conviction was heavy on my heart, the love for things spoke louder than the voice of reason and the voice of my loved ones who were in ministry. I plotted and strategized; thinking I could outsmart the system and for a while I did, or so I thought. I was not a drinker, nor did I smoke cigarettes or marijuana. The majority of my money was spent on looking good, smelling good and being a hero to those that I took care of. After God warned me several times and in his mercy offered me a means of escape, I still continued to do what I wanted. The life I lived was very dangerous and I saw much damage done to the family and friends that lost loved ones.

My oldest daughter was 10 years old and this particular Friday night she was showcasing in a talent show that I was to oversee at her elementary school. I received a call that evening with an opportunity that I could not pass up; an opportunity to get a lot of money for a job that was too smooth to pass up, and in my lustful thinking I wasn't going to pass it up. So, I asked my mom to go to the school and take my place because I had something to do. I remember my mom getting so upset with me this night; I kissed her, laughed and went to my room to put my "fly girl" on. I was preparing myself for the evening. That night, my mom's house was raided and the illegal contents were a huge amount and enough to send me away for a while. I remember looking into my mom's eyes and seeing the disappointment. The police stated that if she didn't tell who the drugs and guns belonged to that she was the one that would be going to jail. She didn't tell, but I did. There was no way I was allowing my mom to go to jail. I was released on an I-bond and I fought the case receiving only a small slap on the wrist– 1 year of probation.

You would have thought it was enough, but that money was coming in so fast; it's like an addiction. I thought about some things and went back to square one, strategizing, trying to figuring out a new way to do what I had to. It lasted for a while. A year later, I was back in the same situation but this time, it wasn't so easy. I was visiting someone's house and it was raided while I was there and the same arresting officer was so excited he made it his business to take everything he found and rest it upon my lap. I was so angry screaming, "I am innocent." Of course, he didn't care and this occurrence landed me in jail again with an unthinkable bond and finally I was placed on house arrest. Six months later, the end result was a prison sentence of 2yrs.

The in between stages of the house arrest and fighting in court was overwhelming and took a great toll on my family. I remember pleading with the attorney to talk to the state and the judge. My sentencing went from eight years to six years and finally down to two years. I was told by the judge, "You have played long enough, take the 2 years or go to trial; if you lose I will give you the maximum time the case carried 6-30 years." Of course, I cried and asked if I could have some time to think about it; she said, "Absolutely not. Take the time and I will give you 60 days to get your affairs in order." So, in June of 1993 I was sentenced to 2 years in prison and was given sixty days to get my affairs in order and turn myself in.

On August 26, 1993, I entered the courtroom with over 75 people (family and friends). With tears in my eyes and theirs, I was turning myself over to the courts. When my name was called and I approached the bench. The judge asked was there anyone there for me. And 90% of the courtroom stood up, the judge told me to look behind me; she asked "who are all those people." I replied most of them are my family the others friends; my parents, Godparents, siblings and others. I remember the look upon the judge's face even to this day.

These are words that wrung in my ears: "There is no reason that you should be here. I judge cases and sentence people daily and I've never seen love and support this strong. It is apparent that you were just doing something, you have no excuse." She looked at them and me again and said, "Verna, look me in the eye. If I ever see you in my courtroom again, I will throw the book at you." I felt so ashamed and embarrassed; it was truly a day of reckoning for me.

I was forced to see myself in a way that didn't paint a pretty picture of who I truly was. I was selfish, unconcerned, and self-absorbed. In this whole process of doing me, I never took the time to think or notice what I was doing to my children, parents and others. My actions not only affected me but generations.

I remember crying in my cell, no longer because I was locked up, but because I was forcing my family to endure a prison term with me. I left my children; I put my mom in a position where she had to raise my children. My dad blamed himself for not being there with us. I was a forced to come to grips with what I needed to do and that was to change my life. My time in prison was like a cave of reality.

I cried and asked God to forgive me and help me to get my life together. I told God that if he would just take care of my family, my parents and children that I would do better. I wouldn't touch drugs again.

God, in his faithfulness, went into immediate action on my behalf. Because I didn't have a high school diploma, it was mandatory that you take the ABE test, (Adult Basic Education Test) to see the level of education that you had. The question was asked of me, "Would you like to get your G.E.D?" and I said, "Yes." Because of my placement scores, I was given an opportunity to immediately take the G.E.D. test without attending classes.

I took the test without prep or studying but God saw me through. If you know anything about G.E.D testing, a portion of that test is based on your writing skills so I was required to write a 300-word essay and the topic of the essay was determined by me pulling a piece of paper out of a box. God's sense of humor is amazing. When I pulled the piece of paper my essay topic was

"If there is anything I could do differently, what would it be?"

I viewed it as another amazing move of God or a sick joke on their part. That question was a no-brainer.

"I WOULDN'T BE HERE, I WOULDN'T BE IN PRISON," and I wrote about that as passionately as I could. The end result of this was that I passed the test and because I scored well, I was given six months good time; that time afforded me an early release date. On October 26th I was placed on a train and sent home on parole. 61 days…. ☺

It's amazing how even in the midst of things that God is mindful and protects you. While in prison for that short time, several dramatic, life-changing events happened. Several of my friends were killed in acts of gang violence and raids. I think I lost approximately six friends within a 60-day period. While I was fighting a case, the guy that I was with was sentenced to 56 years in prison. One thing I had a lot of time to do while incarcerated was to reevaluate my life and to be grateful to God for His mercy and grace towards me. It could've been me too that my family had to bury.

"What the enemy meant for your bad, God will turn it around for your good." Forever grateful for the opportunity to testify about it now and not walk in shame and blame, I vowed never to sale drugs or dip in the lifestyle again and although several opportunities presented it, I was not moved. I resisted and was true to my words.

God, being who He is, blessed me by causing a legal aid office to stumble up on a case that I was denied eight years prior to and they won this case and I was awarded $40,000 and went from making $3.00 an hour on a part-time job to being presented with a interview for a $8.00/hr. position. After that interview, I walked away with a full-time position making $10/hr. + commission, my first real job. Within three years, I was making $35,000-$42,000, give or take annually with continual promotion. I was the first black supervisor in the department, the young grandma, uneducated, black, female, convicted felon, making just as much money as the management team with degrees. God's favor was with me, and He favored me among men. For that I will forever be grateful.

DEFAULT STATUS

I was having trouble with my PC; it would complete the process of loading up, but whenever I clicked on icons or documents, it would freeze and the hourglass would just spin, spin, and spin some more, driving me crazy. I went into panic mode thinking, "Lord, all my business information is on this PC. My contracts; logos; invoices; pictures of all my babies; families, and my work; at least 8 years worth of family memories and other things." I shut it down, waited a few minutes and went through the process again... Same response... JESUS!!! My stuff!! So, I left it running in hopes that the stupid hourglass would give up and stop spinning. I went on to bed and the next morning I got up and went into my office. GUESS WHAT? The hourglass was still spinning, from 10:33 p.m. until that present time, 7:00 a.m. You know how I knew what time it was? The time was displayed on the computer, when the computer froze, so did time. So I went into brain storm mode. "Ok, Jesus, do you think I can get someone to save my files?" I called PC DOC... just to look at the computer was $150, no guarantees about recovering my documents. "Okay, yeah not going to happen. I need to figure out another way." In the

process of all this, I'm thinking, I should've purchased an external hard drive because I had
too much stuff on this computer, too much to lose. Then I thought about a brother at church that works on computers, called his wife, explained the issue and that I needed the brother to come help. When I finally see them together, he says he would come check it out and we set something up. I explained the importance of just wanting the important docs and pictures. We discussed the possibility of lost docs and that frightened me. Oh no, I can't lose my grandbaby's baby pictures. I'm saving those so that when they reach stages of life (high school, college or married) I can create them a "precious moment" album. DEFAULT STATUS. I will have to buy the software Adobe photoCS3. Oh my God, it's about $400. I mentally added up all the photo programs and DVD programs that I purchased to enhance my business, I was sick. Few days went by no calls, no visits, and it's time to brain storm again. I began to think, "Verna what has changed in the recent weeks? What in your normal routine changed?" As I thought about it, I thought about how I had attempted to download a program that someone suggested so that I could get free audio books

and PDF books. So I began to play around with the computer very nervously but curious by nature. I love gadgets so I began to experiment and finally was able to get into the programs and uninstalled that particular application. "NOTE: WARNING! By uninstalling this program feature, you can lose all data saved, do you want to continue?" OH NO! I literally jumped up and ran out the room, willing myself not to continue. I went into the living room, sat on the couch and forced myself to focus elsewhere for a while but it kept coming back to me. So finally I decided to put my big girl pants on and go for it and clicked "Continue". "NOTE: This process can take up to 2 hours." WHAT!!! No instant gratification. I was still forced to wait. I had to wait to see if it worked. If I lost everything, what would I have to work with? Should I have just paid the pros? Jesus, help me. So, I had no other choice but to wait. Finally I came back and the computer read, "RESTART to get the updates." After restarting the computer, and with much fear and trembling, I searched the programs to see what I lost, and to my surprise I hadn't lost anything or so I thought. I checked my pictures they were all there. I checked the programs that I paid mad money for and they were all there; and I was able to operate the PC as though nothing happened, until I decided I wanted to hear some music. When I went to Windows Media to find the album of choice, IT WAS EMPTY; over 500 albums, no songs, albums and sermons that I've collected over the years. I set down on the floor and not one tear would fall. I began to laugh and think about all the stress that I had gone through about this computer. And then I thought, "What if life was like that?"

Sometimes we get so frustrated with life, the program, the setup, just existing. What if we could uninstall the programs that were installed in our life? Those that have given some kind of virus that caused us to slow down, not function properly, or not at all. If we RESTART, what would be left intact or still operational? I thought about all of that. "Do I really want the setting of my life to go back to the DEFAULT status?" I would lose everything; my hard drive would be wiped clean. My answer was "No." I don't want to lose my childhood memories; mom and grandma cooking in the kitchen, teaching me how to bake; memories of knowing my dad was home by the sound of his voice as he would approach the house singing; all the Christmas' that I was extremely satisfied with because everything on my list was under the tree. The story of life lessons told; those monumental events; graduations; first kiss, first car; the birth of my children; birth of my grandchildren. Although some of the events were premature, nevertheless, I love them.

Imagine being empty; to be standing face to face with people that love you and you have no recognition of who they are. Imagine having skill sets that you were born with, or paid money to acquire and now you have zero knowledge of it. Well, I shared this with you because there have been times when we made statements, decrees, and vows, wishing and asking for some of these very things. The truth of the matter is that although I've had some very devastating, dramatic, traumatic events in my life, the good really outweighs the bad. It's just that the BAD was bad and was more impactful than many of our precious moments.

It's so easy to get frustrated with the cares of life. It's so easy to make verbal declarations of, "I wish I could start over" or "I wish I could start over, again" when the truth of the matter is that our life experiences should have purpose. When we know and grow, when we get the understanding of how we operate, then we can troubleshoot our life, debug and perhaps get an anti-virus program to protect and warn us.

Some of what I've said may sound comical. It might even cause alarms to ring in your head. With majority of electronic devices there are instructions and sometimes some assembling may be required. The make and model, most definitely, will require specific components, and maintenance. Well, the same goes for us. We have a maker, someone who has created a massive quantity of human beings, animals, plants (all things). He knows our makeup; He's the master manufacturer and instructions, directions, strategies for life have been provided for us in His word.

We need to take the time to read the manual and do the necessary updates as required. That's how it can be with God but because we can be so frustrated and impatient until we forget who's who, let's go back to the basics. When we try to take short cuts in life, we risk the chance of occurring spiritual viruses; things that come into our life that causes us to be stagnant, function from a place of arrested development, revert to old patterns, to run from purpose and promise. Wishing we were back in default status.

Default: pre-set option, fail to pay, fail to complete, lack of something, fail to appear. Just look at that for minute. Words that are associated with default either fail or lack. NO default status for us. We need to get back to the basic foundations of things and seek God's guidance for provision and a clean slate. Lord, don't make me over, yet create in me a clean heart and renew the right spirit in me. Our journey should be that I won't look back any longer but I will purpose to stay in the press

GROWING

I was thinking about all the times that I cried out and prayed to God to help me grow, mature, and develop in the things of him; making vows to be more like Christ. I know that it's easy to speak about maturing and growing; the fact of the matter is that it's not always an easy process.

When I was young and my body was going through its' stages of growth and development, I remember telling my grandmother that I was sore here and aching there, she would rub me and say it's all a part of growing; she called them growing pains. I remember thinking how many times do I have to grow in this particular area because I don't like the feel of it. Now that I am an adult, I can really reflect on some of the conversations I've had in my youth and that have caused roots and shaped the way I dealt with so many things in my life.

I am a person that loves words. I have a friend whose vocabulary is so extensive; I have to pull out a dictionary to figure out what she is talking about. It was her natural way of dialoguing. I was intrigued by it and often made jokes to her about being a walking grammar girl. I would ask her what did something mean and she would give me a simple synonym for the word(s) and I would bust up laughing and say, "Why didn't you just say that?" She would laugh back and say, "I did." I'm telling you this for a reason. After these encounters, I would hear words that sounded foreign to me. I would look them up and over a period of time when words are spoken it was like this internal alarm that sounds within me that made me seek the definition and question the person's motives or intent when they said it.

I remember a sister who used to always call me hostile; this was a sister that I love and I know she loves me. She would not only call me hostile but said it in a group setting more than once.

One day it really rubbed me the wrong way, so I searched the dictionary for the meaning. Here's what I found: Hostile - very unfriendly, against, relating to enemy, adverse; and some of the synonyms are: antagonistic, aggressive, intimidating, unfriendly, unreceptive, and unsympathetic.

I was alarmed and saddened immediately thinking if this is me then I've been living a lie and my walk is in vein. There is absolutely nothing nice or positive in the characteristic of a hostile individual.

I began to ask people who I know and others that I love, "Do you think that I am unfriendly, unreceptive, unsympathetic?" And the majority said no. I asked some, "Do you think I am antagonistic, aggressive and intimidating?" With the majority, the answer was, "Until one gets to know you, you can appear aggressive and intimidating but not antagonistic."

Let me tell you that I had to do a self-assessment and really seek to know me. I was tweaking! It was painful and I cried out to God and asked for the necessary adjustments and asked God to deal with her heart so she wouldn't say that to me anymore.

Well, one day I was in church and the sister said it again, "You are so hostile!!!!!!!!!" In shock, I didn't say anything. I thought that God and I had an understanding and that He had taken care of this for me. I was forced to assess it again. However, at that moment I realized that aggression will come to play if I address it now, so I will chill right now. I began to feel a wedge between my sister and me, one I didn't want nor could I afford. I called a leader to share with her this place I was in and why. Her counsel to me was, "You must tell her, before bitterness sets in and it can't be repaired."

I slept on it and the next day I sent her an email stating that I don't like it when she called me hostile. I attached the meanings and synonyms and said the reality of it was that word was not connected to my personality, but was stirring up anger that could potentially ruin a relationship that I wanted and needed with her. Of course, at first she was hurt because it wasn't her intent. It wasn't properly used and she is a teacher by nature. The word was used by habit form.

She apologized, sincerely, and I cried with relief. I am grateful for this place in God that I am in. I pray without ceasing for continual growth. As I was writing on this topic of growth, my heart bubbled up with gratefulness thinking about how years ago I would have verbalized my feeling without thinking about hers or the relationship. I would have given her a piece of my mind and not cared if we ever spoke again. Oh, Lord, thank you for Mercy and Grace. I celebrate in knowing that the ending of this was not negative.

PRACTICE WHAT YOU PREACH

Six months later I had a family gathering and I was in the kitchen with my cousin-in-law, a woman that I love, honor and admire dearly. I was forced to deal with a similar situation this time, I was not the victim, I was the one challenged with dealing with my habit forms; the common words I use are "PUNK" and "SHUT UP."

We were joking about something and I called her a punk. And she said, "I love you very much but you are going to stop calling me a punk and telling me to shut up too, it's just rude." I was stung, hurt and speechless because I didn't mean it that way. "Punk" is a word or term of endearment; "shut up" has various meanings and, to me, when I use them, it's not always in a negative content. At that moment I couldn't even apologize, the awkward moment past and we continued to enjoy the evening.

Periodically during the evening, it hit me and I was force to deal with it, which was a growing pain, so I looked up the word and wow.
Punk: an offensive term for a young man regarded as worthless, lazy, or arrogant, an offensive term for a

young gay partner of an older man, no good. The synonyms for punk: none

I prayed for the right words to go to her and the next morning I text her

ME: Thanking you for calling me out on my bad habits, it stung a little but was received with love... I'm working on it.

HER: Oh Verna, I'm sorry it wasn't to hurt you. I love you very much. I just notice you say that a lot when you talk to me and I don't like it. I just think it's very rude. Love hugs and kisses!!!

ME: I know you didn't say it to hurt me, in fact I know that when you say you love me, it is real... Growing pains come with positive growth. People confess all the time that I want to grow, mature, and change. When the challenge and opportunity comes if we are not careful offense will come and make us miss the opportunity to grow. I'm saying to you that I didn't miss this great opportunity to mature. I care about spoken words, they can shape ones destiny, this is a positive thing and I don't want to be rude especially to people I love, honor, and respect.

HER: K......

HER: I enjoyed you all yesterday and thanks for sharing your family.

Now, here's the part I want you all to get. My cousin is one of the most loving people I know; one that honors and respects my walk with God and goes out of her way to respect the God in me when I'm around. She is someone that will verbalize her love for God but she does not go to church. This situation was a growing experience for me to make me shift in my thinking. She cared more about OUR relationship than my dysfunctional habit and called me out on it. I'm grateful to her for that.

I'm saying, too often in the growing process we will face or encounter people that will show us or challenge us to shift in some or several areas of life and if we are not careful, we will allow pride, ignorance, or offense to blind us of the awesomeness of growth and development. Let's embrace the necessary change and adhere to it. It's one of those achievements that if it has a domino effect, imagine how much better and productive we would be if such a change hit all of our hearts.

Extraordinary wouldn't you say?

FORGIVENESS

Forgiveness

- To grant pardon for or remission of an offense, debt, etc. resolve
- To give up all claims on account of remit
- To grant pardon to a person
- To cease to feel resentment against

Synonyms: accept pardon, commute, dismiss from mind, kiss and make up, overlook, and to let it pass I'll start with this: God's awesomeness exceeds my ability to comprehend. This is not one of those topics that is typically laid out on the "Let's talk about it" table discussions. In most cases, it's not an easy subject matter, especially when you are the one who is faced with forgiving. When I completed (or thought I completed) this book, I felt as though something was missing. I couldn't put my finger on it, I was not satisfied with it. *It felt incomplete.* One week while preparing for the women's prayer meeting at church, I spent the last few days seeking God for a strategy and God placed it upon my heart to pray for Grace. As I researched **Grace**, one of the definitions was: *A capacity to tolerate, accommodate, and forgive people.* So, I prayed about the grace to forgive and move forward. That night in prayer, I felt that thing in my soul and I now know that what I felt was my soul's cry to release them. Release everyone that you are holding hostage with your inability to REALLY forgive.

We often say that we forgive and on the majority we have every intention of doing just that. It's just that sometimes the wounds are so deep, the nature and the act of the things tend to overrule our verbal declaration of, "I forgive. I forgive her. I forgive him." Often times we must forgive ourselves.

Mark 11:25 Whenever you stand praying, forgive.

Matthew 6:14-15 Forgive those that trespass against you.

Luke 17:3-4 Pay attention to yourself; if your brother sins, rebuke him and if he repents forgive him, no matter how often he sins if he repents, forgive him.

The best example I can think of, biblically, about a true demonstration of forgiveness outside of Jesus' forgiving is the story of Stephen's stoning. In the book of Acts, it says, "As the people stoned Stephen... he cried out 'forgive them they are so blinded by their religion, culture, and tradition. They don't realize the sins; they don't understand the consequences of their actions." (Acts 7:59-60 My translation)

Man that was something powerful for Stephen to release. In the midst of being stoned to death he cared about the people being pardon versus an eye for an eye, a tooth for a tooth. His cry wasn't one of "Avenge me, Lord" but "Lord, forgive them." Now that's one to Selah on. Can you imagine the state the world would be if all victims prayed that prayer in the midst of being violated, wronged, lied on, abused, etc.?

On Thanksgiving morning, I was in Worship and one of the sisters released a song about the woman at the well, "AFTER THE DRINK." What happened after the drink? She thirst no more; she couldn't contain her excitement. She had to go tell about the man she met at the well, who knew things about her that no one else did. That sparked something in me and I began to scribe, writing down the words as fast as they entered my thoughts.

As I was writing, a brother took over the worship and declared that forgiveness is the key. He began to state, "If you are going to feel the reign of God's presence over you, then we must take off the garment of un-forgiveness." He also said, "Get someone in mind. Someone that you know that you have to forgive… your parents, yourself, siblings, whoever that person might be, get them in your mind and release them for good and for real."

At that moment a light bulb went off. I thought about the person that violated me sexually and I thought it strange that my natural response wasn't to become emotional and cry. I felt strong and free, for the first time in my life. I felt the anger and un-forgiveness being unlinked from my heart; still no tears just an overwhelming urge to write the story.

Yes, it was the missing part to the Journey! It is the finale to the Journey and could not have been written prior to this experience.

After service one of my sisters asked me to go over to my dad's house with her. When we got there, we were laughing and talking with my dad and his wife and all of the suddenly he walked in. (The molester, the violator) Me: *looking like a deer in headlights, I did an internal scream.* He walked around the room greeting everyone with hugs and kisses. In the past, I the woman of God who was declaring

"I am whole," never failed to explode internally in response to his mere presence. Like a predator, I waited for someone to ask me why I didn't like him so that I could reveal that he's a molester, a sexual predator, a violator of covenant and trust.

How was it that I was able to crucify him without a second thought? I'll tell you how. Hurt people look to hurt others and I demonstrated that as often as I could. My inability to forgive him was more painful than the hurt of the actions. I was still as effected as the little girl that had been violated all those many years ago. My hurt and un-forgiveness said "expose and uncover him no matter what." I didn't even care about who was going to be effected. In my mind, I felt like I protected my parents from it when I was young. Now that I released that, I don't have to. Let the pain begin. And not once did he defend himself or even call me a lie. He simply called me mean and so did others.

But on this particular day, this last encounter, I didn't react; I didn't slap him, kick him and tell him I hate him; I didn't push him off me. With all my mixed emotions I extended by heart to forgive and embraced him back. I even asked him could I pray for him and I did. I said a simple prayer with my hand on his knees. Those in the room that know the history were paralyzed; they were waiting on the explosion to happen. Even my dad, in a subtle way, was trying to divert his attention elsewhere. I even asked him to sing for me. I had a sense of peace and realized one thing like never before. We do not wrestle against flesh and blood. (Ephesians 6:12) I realized for the first time, even after hearing and reading that scripture on countless times, that I have to forgive; that I have in fact forgiven him.

Upon the departure, my dad hugged me very tight and the unspoken words spoke volume. He was affirming how proud he was of me for moving from a place of anger and pain; a place that I wrestled with for years.

Forgiving someone, even yourself, will only be done when you walk out God's Grace from a place of demonstration and not just declaration. I can now tell you this because I'm finally there and no longer is it a nightmare, but a testimony of a father's love. Sister(s) I don't know in which area it is that you are unable to forgive. It may be your father, mother, siblings, family member, friend, spouse, or child.

Your story might not be my story but one thing I know for sure is whatever state of un-forgiveness that you may have, it is not the will of God and it most definitely hinders the process for your promise in God. You must forgive. You must let go; not for the person or people, but so that the shackles of that thing can be broken off and the key to it is releasing it and moving forward.

I have truly forgiven the demon of molestation/rape. I have made a decree to pray for his total deliverance and healing in the mind.

My God is awesome and forever lives to give intercession on my behalf.

Prayer For forgiveness

Father God,
I thank you for your Grace, the capacity to tolerate and forgive people. I pray that the inability to forgive is no longer my portion; it cannot and will not hold me active and stop me from the destiny that God has set before me. I pray that as you continue to create in me a clean heart and renew the right spirit within me that, according to Matthew 6:14, if I forgive men when they sin against me you, my Heavenly Father, will also forgive me. I recognize that failure to forgive leaves me without forgiveness from you Lord according to Matthew 6:15.
I decree that my declaration to forgive in not only a verbal declaration but also that of my heart. All deep wounds of the past that try to surface when restoration and reconciliation should be taking place have no voice or rule in my walk with you, Lord.
I renounce all spirits of religion, cultures and traditions that have subtly spoken volumes about others that have caused me hurt, pain, disappointment, viewed them wicked and unjust and not worthy of forgiveness. I thank you Lord that when the spirit is willing and the flesh is weak that I am strengthened in your presence to walk as an heir of promise and wholeness, where there is nothing broken or anything missing.

I understand that forgiveness is the key to walking in total liberation and liberation that comes from dwelling in the secret place of the most high according to Psalm 91. Today, I put on the garment of forgiveness and I release those that I hold un-forgiveness towards and myself. [If you have a person/people in mind, verbally release them, say their name]. I let you go for real and free my heart to express the love and the will of God. I will no longer release words and expose others because I am hurt and feel victimized but I will seek your counsel for guidance and instructions.

I now realize that my inability to forgive has been more painful than the action done. I speak wholeness to my heart, mind and emotions. I am not a victim. I am an Heir of the righteous from this day forward I extend my heart to walk in forgiveness and I trust the leading of your spirit to carry me through this journey of becoming total and free from shame, blame, hatred, bitterness, pain, and disappointments. I will no longer walk in uncertainty due to the dysfunctions of my past. I am crucified with Christ, according to Galatians 2:20. From this day forward I am walking with a heart of love and compassion. From this day forward I am free because I have totally forgiven and the bondage and weight is no longer my portion. I walk in healing, peace, and joy because the spirit of un-forgiveness is completely cancelled and no longer resides in my heart in Jesus name.

"I beseech you therefore by the mercy of God to be intentional about changing". It is most definitely easier said than done but the reward of freedom is worth all the uneasy feelings that you are facing. Remember this: a lesson not learned is a lesson repeated. Whatever the lesson is or was make sure you learn from it so that you won't have to repeat viscous cycles of hurt, pain, disappointment and your inability to forgive.

Be free!

"Knowledge is KEY,
But applied Knowledge is POWER"
Apply what you've learned
and those things that you can relate to
and embrace it.

Pastor Verna Steele

New Beginning

I welcome feedback regarding this book. Feel free to email me at TheJourney_tatw@yahoo.com

You are destined for greatness

Blessings, healing, and wholeness to you all…

Pastor Verna Steele